JUDICIAL BRANCH

by Vincent Alexander

po go

Ideas for Parents and Teachers

Pogo Books let children practice reading informational text while introducing them to nonfiction features such as headings, labels, sidebars, maps, and diagrams, as well as a table of contents, glossary, and index.

Carefully leveled text with a strong photo match offers early fluent readers the support they need to succeed.

Before Reading

- "Walk" through the book and point out the various nonfiction features. Ask the student what purpose each feature serves.
- Look at the glossary together. Read and discuss the words.

Read the Book

- Have the child read the book independently.
- Invite him or her to list questions that arise from reading.

After Reading

- Discuss the child's questions. Talk about how he or she might find answers to those questions.
- Prompt the child to think more. Ask: What did you know about the judicial branch of the government before you read this book? What more do you want to learn about this branch?

Pogo Books are published by Jump!
5357 Penn Avenue South
Minneapolis, MN 55419
www.jumplibrary.com

Copyright © 2019 Jump!
International copyright reserved in all countries. No part of this book may be reproduced in any form without written permission from the publisher.

Library of Congress Cataloging-in-Publication Data

Names: Alexander, Vincent, author.
Title: Judicial branch / Vincent Alexander.
Description: Minneapolis, MN : Jump!, Inc., 2018.
Series: My Government | Includes index.
Audience: Age 7-10.
Identifiers: LCCN 2017056998 (print)
LCCN 2017054678 (ebook) | ISBN 9781624969331 (e-book) | ISBN 9781624969317 (hardcover : alk. paper) | ISBN 9781624969324 (pbk.)
Subjects: LCSH: Courts–United States–Juvenile literature. | Justice, Administration of–United States–Juvenile literature.
Classification: LCC KF8700 (print) | LCC KF8700 .A94 2018 (ebook) | DDC 347.73/1–dc23
LC record available at https://lccn.loc.gov/2017056998

Editor: Kristine Spanier
Book Designer: Leah Sanders

Photo Credits: r.classen/Shutterstock, cover; Image Source/iStock, 1; Chris Ryan/iStock, 3; Two Bridges Photography/Shutterstock, 4; Andrey_Popov/Shutterstock, 5; Erik Cox Photography/Shutterstock, 6-7; Heidi Benser/Getty, 8-9; Alina555/Getty, 10; moodboard/Getty, 11; Marmaduke St. John/Alamy, 12-13; Saul Loeb/Getty, 14; The Washington Post/Getty, 15; alancrosthwaite/iStock, 16-17; eurobanks/Shutterstock, 18-19; Rena Schild/Shutterstock, 20-21; Michael Ventura/Alamy, 23.

Printed in the United States of America at Corporate Graphics in North Mankato, Minnesota.

TABLE OF CONTENTS

CHAPTER 1

NATION OF LAWS

Three branches form the U.S. government. The legislative branch makes **laws**. The executive branch enforces them. What does the judicial branch do?

It decides if laws are fair. Or if they have been broken. Many courts make up this branch. The Supreme Court is the top court.

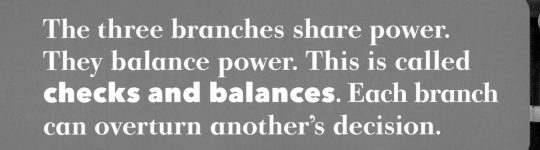

The three branches share power. They balance power. This is called **checks and balances**. Each branch can overturn another's decision.

Supreme Court Courtroom

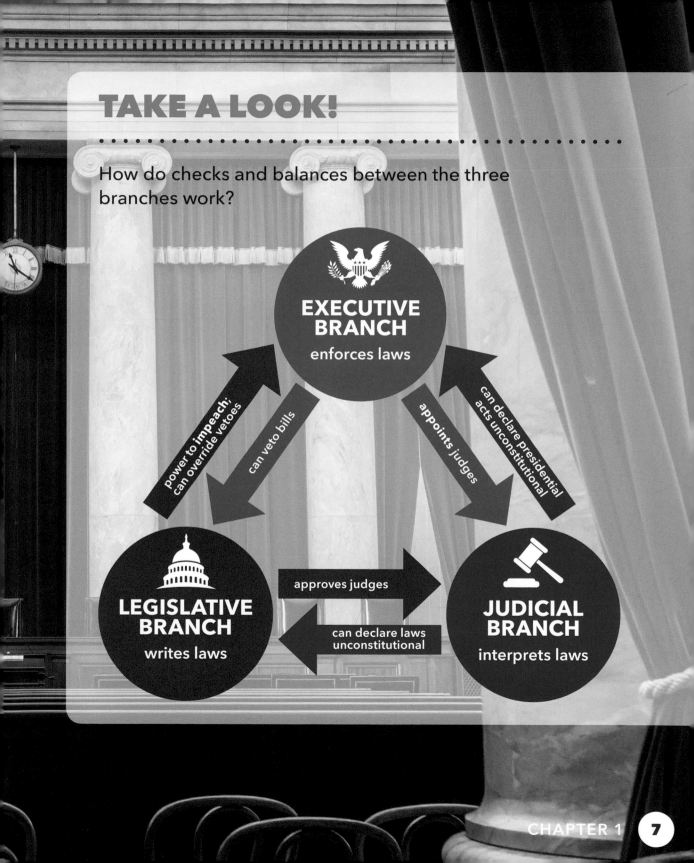

TAKE A LOOK!

How do checks and balances between the three branches work?

EXECUTIVE BRANCH
enforces laws

power to impeach; can override vetoes

can veto bills

appoints judges

can declare presidential acts unconstitutional

LEGISLATIVE BRANCH
writes laws

approves judges

can declare laws unconstitutional

JUDICIAL BRANCH
interprets laws

Federal courts deal mostly with civil law. Civil law involves disagreements. Has a business deal been broken? Does someone owe money? These cases can be **settled** in state courts. Or they might move to a federal court.

CHAPTER 2

MANY COURTS

When does a trial move to a federal district court? If the people in **dispute** do not live in the same state. Or a federal law has been broken. Or a person's rights have been **violated**.

jury

A trial has a judge and a **jury**.
The jury decides who is right.
Those who lose may **appeal**. How?
The case moves to a higher court.

U.S. Courts of Appeals are higher than district courts. They have more judges. But there is no jury. The judges may change the lower court's decision.

And if they don't? There is just one more court of appeal.

DID YOU KNOW?

U.S. Courts of Appeals are also known as circuit courts.

CHAPTER 3

THE SUPREME COURT

The Supreme Court is the highest court. It has nine **justices**. The president appoints them. The **Senate** approves the choices. They are justices for life.

Supreme Court justices

They take two oaths. They promise to be fair. And they promise to defend the U.S. Constitution.

The Constitution is a written document. It describes the government's powers. And our rights. These include our basic freedoms. Like what? Speech. Religion. And freedom of the **press**. The justices pick cases that may affect these.

The justices **hear** cases. They do research. They meet to discuss. A majority must agree on each decision.

TAKE A LOOK!

How does a case get to the Supreme Court?

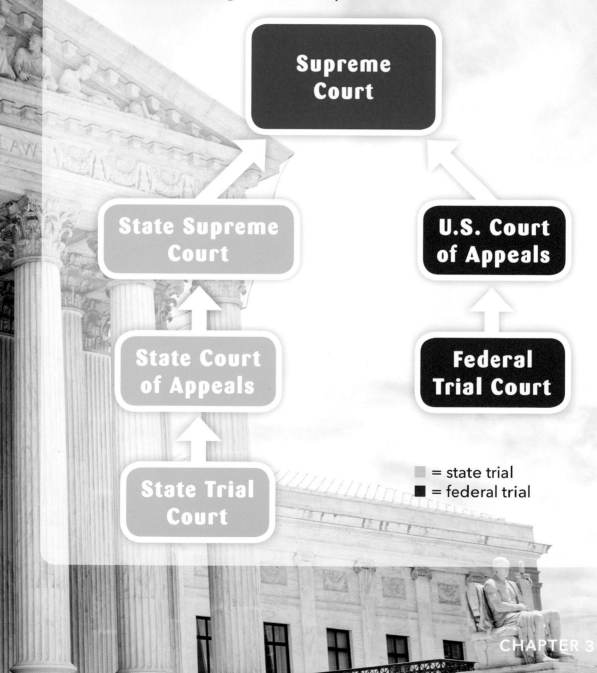

Supreme Court

State Supreme Court

U.S. Court of Appeals

State Court of Appeals

Federal Trial Court

State Trial Court

■ = state trial
■ = federal trial

The Supreme Court has decided many important cases. They have changed how we live. For example, they decided separate schools based on race is wrong. Marriage is now a right for all people.

What is the Supreme Court working on now? Find out! It might change history.

DID YOU KNOW?

Each year, about 7,500 cases are sent to the Supreme Court. How many do the justices hear? Usually only about 150!

ACTIVITIES & TOOLS

CONDUCT A MOCK TRIAL

Find a court case in the news. Read both sides. Tell your family about it. Appoint one member of your family to be the judge. Choose which side of the case you want to argue. Have another family member take the other side.

Now take turns presenting your side of the case to the judge. Have the judge ask you questions. Answer them. Give the judge time to reach a decision. Did you win? Was your argument better? Was the decision fair?

Continue to follow the trial in the news. Find out which side wins. Is it the same outcome as your mock trial? Do you agree with the decision? If the decision is appealed, keep following the case in the news. What court does it go to next?

GLOSSARY

appeal: To apply to a higher court for a change in a legal decision.

appoints: Chooses someone for a job or position.

checks and balances: A system that ensures one branch of the government is not more powerful than the other branches.

dispute: A disagreement about an issue.

federal: The central power of the United States.

hear: To give a listening to legal arguments in a case.

impeach: To formally charge a public official with misconduct.

jury: A group of people, usually 12 in number, who listen to the facts at a trial and decide whether the accused person is guilty or innocent.

justices: The people in charge of the Supreme Court who decide the matters brought to the court.

laws: Rules made and enforced by a government.

press: The journalists and the organizations that collect, publish, and broadcast the news.

Senate: One of the two houses of the U.S. Congress that makes laws.

settled: Decided or agreed on something.

violated: To have broken a rule or law.

INDEX

TO LEARN MORE

Learning more is as easy as 1, 2, 3.

1) Go to www.factsurfer.com
2) Enter "judicialbranch" into the search box.
3) Click the "Surf" button to see a list of websites.

With factsurfer, finding more information is just a click away.